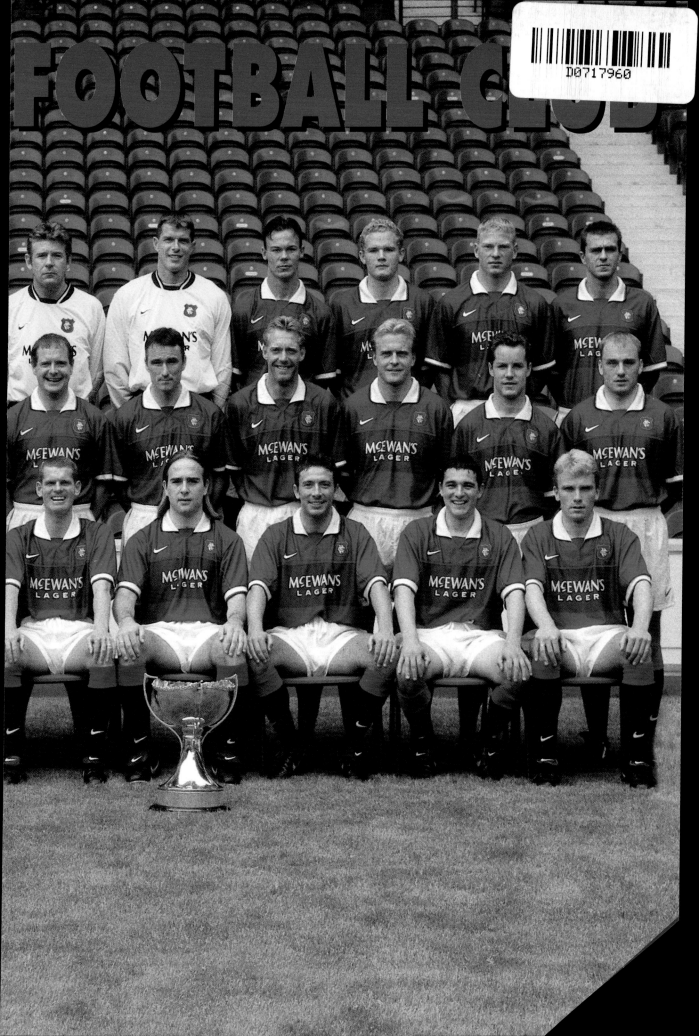

FOOTBALL CLUB

D0717960

Who's who at Ibrox

CHAIRMAN
David Murray

VICE CHAIRMAN
Donald R. Findlay

DIRECTOR/SECRETARY
Campbell Ogilvie

DIRECTORS
Hugh R.W. Adam
Daniel Levy
Jim MacDonald
Ian B. Skelly
Howard Stanton

DIRECTOR/MANAGER
Walter Smith

CLUB CAPTAIN
Brian Laudrup

COMMERCIAL MANAGER
Bob Reilly

Rangers captain Brian Laudrup with the championship trophy

Roll of honour

EUROPEAN CUP WINNERS' CUP WINNERS
1972

SCOTTISH LEAGUE CHAMPIONS
1891, 1899, 1900, 1901,
1902, 1911, 1912, 1913,
1918, 1920, 1921, 1923,
1924, 1925, 1927, 1928,
1929, 1930, 1931, 1933,
1934, 1935, 1937, 1939,
1947, 1949, 1950, 1953,
1956, 1957, 1959, 1961,
1963, 1964, 1975, 1976,
1978, 1987, 1989, 1990,
1991, 1992, 1993, 1994,
1995, 1996, 1997

SCOTTISH CUP WINNERS
1894, 1897, 1898, 1903,
1928, 1930, 1932, 1934,
1935, 1936, 1948, 1949,
1950, 1953, 1960, 1962,
1963, 1964, 1966, 1973,
1976, 1978, 1979, 1981,
1992, 1993, 1996

SCOTTISH LEAGUE CUP WINNERS
1946/47, 1948/49, 1960/61,
1961/62, 1963/64, 1964/65,
1970/71, 1975/76, 1977/78,
1978/79, 1981/82, 1983/84,
1984/85, 1986/87, 1987/88,
1988/89, 1990/91, 1992/93,
1993/94, 1996/97

Designed, edited, published and distributed on behalf of Rangers Football Club by First Press Publishing, 193 Bath Street, Glasgow G2 4HU

WORDS
Michelle Simpson
Keith Jackson
Iain King
Fraser Mackie
Darrell King
7 Day Press

DESIGN & LAYOUT
Kerry Burnett
Bob Steel

PRODUCTION EDITOR
Brian McSweeney

ARTWORK
Robert Chambers

PHOTOGRAPHS
Rob Casey

FIRST PRESS
PUBLISHING

Telephone: 0141 226 2200
Fax: 0141 248 1099

nnual

CONTENTS

THE FIRST HALF

THE SECOND HALF

AND IF YOU'VE GOT ANY EXTRA TIME...

Let Paul Gascoigne take you through a training session in his own unique style, try to complete the Nine-in-a-row quiz, reminisce with Golden moments, check out the Gers' young stars of the future and laugh at the press quotes from the year!

This might be hard to believe. But Brian Laudrup, the European superstar, was just as excited as any other new Rangers fan as he prepared to watch the latest Ibrox video.

Three and a half years ago, the Danish winger was given a couple of tapes from Rangers legend Mark Hateley, to obtain a flavour of the new football world he had entered.

One, *Rangers Gold 2*, already featured the early highlights of Laudrup's destruction of Premier League defences even although he had only played in light blue for two months.

But the footage – amid all the other famous players – which really caught Laudrup's eye was that of a man who had also worn the number 11 jersey with pride.

Laudrup had not heard of Davie Cooper before arriving in a £2.25 million transfer from Fiorentina, but it did not take him long to appreciate his skills.

And when Laudrup sits back in several years time to remember his achievements in a thrilling football career, he will cherish the thought that he will be regarded up there with Cooper, as one of the greatest ever Rangers men.

It is that scenario plus his genuine love for Rangers and total pride in helping the team to win nine-in-a-row that makes Laudrup a caring class apart from most of the foreign players who flood the British game.

"I'm afraid I didn't know anything about Davie Cooper when I arrived," admits Laudrup. "Fortunately, I soon realised because I watched the Gold video myself – I have it at home – and suddenly I saw this wonderfully talented and very skilful player.

"He had an amazing left foot, took on every defender, scored some absolutely cracking goals and was setting up at least the same number of chances for others.

"I said to myself 'Who is that player?' So I asked my father because I thought he might have played at the same time but he didn't know him either. It was strange to see such a good player and not know anything about him.

"I was away with Denmark when Davie Cooper passed away, which was a great tragedy. I realised when I came back what a loss he was to all the Rangers fans and football fans in general.

"It's an honour to be compared to Davie Cooper"

BRI'S TO BE

The Great Dane is kee

WITH BRIAN LAUDRUP

"I saw this wonderfully talented and skilful player"

"I must say I've seen a couple of videos from his games and to be mentioned in the same way is an honour. I feel he must be one of the best ever.

Laudrup is most Rangers fans' favourite of the current era. Without his mazy runs, jet fast pace, remarkable balance and unshakeable coolness in front of goal, the golden period of the Nineties might have been disrupted by a barren championship year.

Long after he leaves, the memory of his greatest moments in blue will warm the hearts of supporters who saw him play – much in the same way that those who grew up or grew old watching Cooper, will recall.

From the minute he began that 50-yard dash to set up a Duncan Ferguson winner against Motherwell on his Scottish debut to the final farewell he bids to his 'We're not worthy' fans in the stands of Ibrox, Laudrup has been a true credit to the club.

Laudrup entered himself into Rangers folklore with the goal that clinched a ninth Premier title in a row to equal Celtic's championship record.

The 28-year-old scored a stunning diving header against Dundee United at Tannadice to secure a 1-0 victory and spark celebrations among Rangers fans that would go on long into the night… and May… and the summer!

Remarkably, Laudrup believes he has only scored four goals with his head throughout the professional football career which started with Brondby.

Turn over for more Brian banter!

DELIGHTED A LEGEND

o Follow Follow Rangers' history

THE BRIAN LAUDRUP INTERVIEW

Continued from page seven

It was a fitting close to a season where Laudrup really earned his wages and worship from the Ibrox legions. As captain in the absence of injured skipper Richard Gough, he assumed more responsibility than ever before.

So when he joined the rest of the squad back in Glasgow that night and saw thousands of joyous fans crowded in Edmiston Drive, it was the finest moment in his club football career.

"If people asked me later what the highlights would be I would name winning the 1992 European Championships with Denmark and also equalling Celtic's record," insists Laudrup.

"I felt a joy that I hadn't felt at any other club. The first two Premier Leagues were special but last season was incredible. To witness about 5000 fans singing and dancing outside Ibrox at two o'clock in the morning was amazing.

"At least I can remember that. The last time I scored a goal with my head was for Fiorentina against Roma and I clashed heads with a defender.

"I never realised I scored and it took me five or 10 minutes to take it in. I watched TV a few days later to remind myself of the goal!

"It will be fantastic when I look back in 10 years at the history books and see myself as the player who scored the vital goal to achieve nine-in-a-row – something that means so much to all Rangers fans.

"I had put myself in the place of a supporter to imagine what it feels like having to hear about Celtic's record of nine for so long.

"Suddenly we were in that position and I was determined to make sure the eight previous years did not count for nothing.

"Perhaps a lot of European players who haven't played in Scotland don't realise what it means to people.

"Well, that's a shame because I feel, as I've said all along, that coming to Rangers was the best move of my career and to win as important a title as that makes all the efforts worth it."

If you've met Brian Laudrup, even if it was just outside the front door of Ibrox while waiting for his autograph, then you probably will believe that watching that old video footage did help along the way to making him a real Ranger.

Now can you wait for the tape marked *The Best Of Brian Laudrup?*

> "It was a joy I'd never felt at any club"

Lauders reflects on the moment that made history

A-HEAD OF THE REST

"I didn't know whether to laugh or cry!"

JUST THE TICKET

"That night at Tannadice was amazing! I'd only missed one game all season and until 45 minutes before kick-off I didn't even have a ticket!

"The feeling when Laudrup powered in that header was beyond belief – I didn't know whether to laugh or cry!

"As I looked around at the sheer joy on all the fans' faces I felt a feeling I'd never experienced before – I'll remember it forever."

JOHN MILLER
DUNDE

A trip round Ibrox Stadium is a top treat for any true blue. From the second you walk up the steps emblazoned with the RFC crest and in the regal doors on Edmiston Drive (1), you can tell you're about to witness something very special.

The imposing hallway (2), is the first port of call as the Ibrox Commissionaire, Peter Jacobs, waits to welcome all visitors – and stop any intruders!

As is expected of a club of Rangers' stature, any waiting guests are kept comfortable in the luxurious waiting room (3), just off the fantastic foyer that is Peter's domain. The walk up the magnificent marble staircase (4) will take any Rangers fan into dreamland as you picture the many

TOUR OF A

5

6

boys in blue that have taken those very steps up to the Boardroom to sign on the dotted line.

At the top of the stairs, is the historic Blue Room (5) – the scene of the Loving Cup Ceremony. After the first home game of every New Year, both boards savour a sip from the cup to toast the reigning British monarch and sing the National Anthem.

Just along the corridor is the jewel in the Ibrox crown – the breathtaking Trophy Room (6).

Filled with a fine array of Rangers trophies and medals and featuring every Championship winning flag in the Gers history, this remarkable room summons up many memorable moments for every Teddy Bear who has the pleasure of visiting it.

TURN OVER FOR ALL ABOUT IBROX

LIFETIME

All you ever wanted to know about

In 1900 Glasgow boasted the three largest football stadia in the world – Ibrox, Parkhead and Hampden.

The grand red brick main stand which runs along Edmiston Drive, with its Lion Rampant shield and 'Aye Ready' motto, was built in 1928. Declared a listed building in 1980 it was the stunning work of top football designer Archibald Leitch whose work can also be spotted at Everton's Goodison Park and Fratton Park, the home of Portsmouth.

Ibrox now boasts a 50,400 capacity making it one of the largest stadiums in Britain – and one of the most valuable worth over £50 million!

Tragically, Ibrox and its supporters have twice faced the devastation of disasters. In 1902, 26 people died at a Scotland-England match when the terracing gave way then, on January 2, 1971, disaster struck once again during an Old Firm game. As thousands of supporters tried to exit the game a crush developed on Stairway 13 of the Copland Road terracing killing 66 people.

Before moving to the current Ibrox Stadium in 1899, the Gers were the nomads of Scottish football. From playing their very first game against Callender FC on the public pitches at Flesher's Haugh on Glasgow Green, the Gers then played at Burnbank near Great Western Road, followed by a 13 year spell at Kinning Park and 2 years at the old Ibrox Park – situated where the ticket office and Edmiston house sit today.

The Copland Road Stand, formerly the east terracing, was the first of the fine new stands to be presented to the public in a 2-2 draw with Celtic in August 1979.

The Ibrox support welcomed Spurs on August 4, 1980, for the official opening of the Broomloan Road Stand while Liverpool were the guests for the unveiling of the Govan Stand on December 22, 1981. It was mixed fortunes for the Gers with a 2-1 win over the Londoners followed by a 2-0 defeat from the reds of Liverpool.

Arsenal visited Ibrox in 1953 for the first ever floodlit match at the stadium. Ibrox also staged the first floodlit Scottish League match when they inflicted an 8-0 defeat on Queen of the South in 1956.

Ibrox hasn't always been a blue heaven! Until the recent renovation the stands were multi-coloured with red, yellow, blue, orange and brown seats!

THE BLUE

the finest stadium in the world...

Hearts were the first team ever to play at Ibrox way back in December, 1899 and the Gers got off to a flying start running out with a 3-1 victory!

On January 2, 1939, a crowd of 118,567 turned out at Ibrox to watch the Light Blues record a 2-1 victory over Old Firm rivals Celtic. To this day, it is the largest crowd ever to attend a league match in Britain.

Previously an oval ground, in 1978 redevelopment began at Ibrox to make it the stadium we know today. Although claimed to be based on Borussia Dortmund's Westfalenstadion which was once described as 'The sort of football arena that all fans dream about' most of the loyal legions who visited the Germans home in the 1995 Champions League tie would agree the Gers' stadium is now far superior.

When the USSR came to Glasgow in 1991 it was the first time in 50 years that Ibrox had hosted a game for the Scottish national side.

It's not all football at Ibrox! Loads of top songsters like Bon Jovi and Rod Stewart have played to sell-out crowds at the ground.

The first European match to be played at Ibrox was on October 24, 1956. French side NIce were the opposition in a 2-1 win for the Gers in the Champions' Cup. Unfortunately the Gers crashed out of the cup after going down 2-1 in the away tie followed by a 3-1 defeat in the play-off in the Parc des Princes in Paris.

The 1899 Ibrox stadium was described as 'the finest football ground in the world' when it opened its doors. With a large two-storey pavillion, a grandstand and a covered enclosure – nicknamed the 'Bovril Stand' because of a Bovril advert on the roof! – it was a slightly different stadium from the one we all frequent now!

HEAVEN

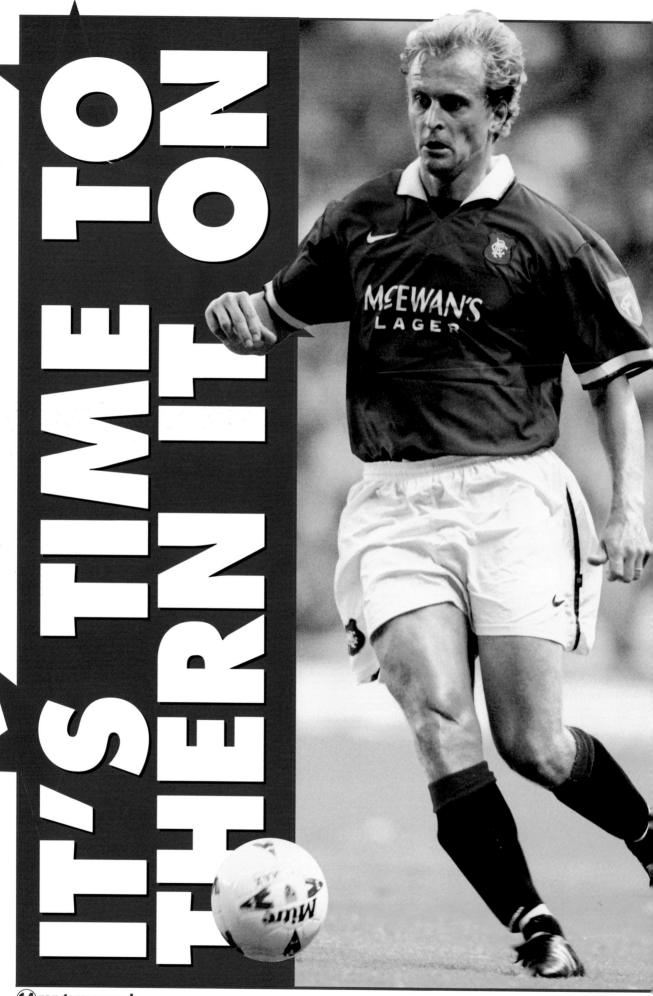

IT'S TIME TO THEN IT ON

Jonas paves the Gers way ahead

No-one would have blamed Jonas Thern for thinking twice about joining Rangers in the summer.

It was not a case of the Scottish champions failing to be an attractive proposition for the stylish Swede.

Instead, he might have shuddered at memories of playing at Ibrox Stadium.

His only appearance at the home of Rangers came in a World Cup encounter with Scotland and it was hardly a memorable occasion for the then Roma midfielder.

"I remember that we put so much into that game and came away with nothing," said Thern.

"We lost 1-0 and dropped three vital points. Yes, I remember well the display of Jim Leighton that afternoon.

"Quite simply, he was unbeatable. We had about three or four opportunities that day but just couldn't get the ball past the Scots goalkeeper."

Thern, thankfully, didn't allow that World Cup reverse to put him off playing his club football in Glasgow.

"Ibrox Stadium is undoubtedly one of the finest in Europe," said the gifted maestro. "If you can't play football on that surface, then you can't play at all."

The Ibrox jigsaw is still coming together and that is only to be expected with so much comings and goings over the past six months.

With a record-equalling nine successive Championships installed in the history books, manager Walter Smith has set about revamping the club.

New players have been introduced after a close season of frenzied transfer activity and Thern was just one of the big names persuaded to ply his trade at Ibrox.

There was massive disappointment on the Champions League front when Rangers lost out to Thern's fellow-Swedes Gothenburg.

However, the international ace has refused to panic. He added: "Rangers are a massive club and must always be seen to be making an impression in the top tournaments.

"Of course, the Gothenburg results upset us but, remember, we were still getting to know each other's styles at the time.

"We do not hide behind excuses, though. We will get better, you can be sure of that."

That's fighting talk from the player who has also played for Varnamo, Malmo, Benfica and Napoli.

And in that sort of mood, Jonas Thern is a fearsome prospect.

"IF YOU CAN'T PLAY FOOTBALL AT IBROX YOU CAN'T PLAY AT ALL"

"When Gough started crying I let it all out!"

CHEERS, TEARS AND SOUVENIRS

"After the downer of the defeat by Motherwell at Ibrox on the Monday, the sight of Richard Gough lifting the trophy at Tannadice was even more emotional than I'd ever anticipated.

"I knew that clinching nine would mean a lot to me – after all I'd listened to Celtic fans going on and on about their great feat for years – but I didn't realise it would be so overwhelming.

"And when Gough started crying that was it – I just had to let it all out too."

DAVE HOLLAND, UDDINGSTON

"did I say that?"

When I stepped forward to receive my ninth straight title trophy with Celtic I thought I was part of something that would never be equalled.

Rangers have proved me wrong and I take my hat off to them.
Billy McNeil, The Sun, May 97

Rangers' decade of domestic domination has run in tandem with almost non-stop disappointment and humiliation in Europe. It has also run in tandem with their ONLY rivals Celtic being in almost constant crisis.

Playing in the Champions League should be Rangers' zenith but on such Ibrox nights you can smell the fear.

That fear is well-founded because Rangers' Euro record since the so-called revolution has been a DISGRACE.
Gerry McNee, Sunday Mail, May 97

Walter Smith's right to fear that Eight (Paul Gascoigne) has tarnished his and the club's image.

Other bosses shake their heads at what the Ibrox club has accepted. Smith should have spoken out long ago.

And how much weight will his words carry if he allows Eight to cavort around Ibrox in a silly hat next Monday when Gers celebrate nine-in-a-row?

Eight's main contribution was stabbing Smith in the back with a Champions League red card against Ajax.
Gerry McNee, Sunday Mail, April 97

Veteran hotshot Ally McCoist had BEGGED Kansas City Wizards to deal him in when he quits Rangers.
Iain McFarlane, Daily Star, April 97

It's great to see a wee club in a semi-final brushing aside the critics and getting a second bite at the cherry.

And it's great to have Falkirk involved again as well!
Ally McCoist expresses his pleasure at Celtic's Scottish Cup Semi-final replay! News of the World, April 97

But if Oasis go on and become the Beatles and have 10 albums that each sell 20 million, it would be great for me to go back and buy Rangers.

I'd get them out of the Scottish League and into the English Premiership. What's wrong with Scottish football is that they need decent opposition. You've got world class – well, great – players like Gascoigne, Laudrup, Goram, McCoist – well McCoist's getting on a bit, nearly the same age as me – but they're playing Raith Rovers four times a year.
Alan McGee, Creation Records' boss (quoted by Sue Mott, Scotland on Sunday)

We have said it before and we make no apology for saying it again:

GAZZA MUST GO. Rangers must bite the bullet and show their flawed genius the door – and the sooner the better.

Paul Gascoigne has betrayed the club, he has betrayed Walter Smith, he has betrayed his dwindling army of fans and he has betrayed Scottish football.
Sun Editorial

Rangers seem to be able to lift themselves for bigger game and, although it pains me to admit it, I think our attitude hasn't always been correct when we've played against some other sides.
Richard Gough, The Express, November 96

Three fire tenders screeched to a halt outside Celtic Park – five minutes too late to turn the cold hoses on Paolo Di Canio after an inferno of an Old Firm game.
Daily Mail's Brian Scott's alternative view of the Old Firm hate game March 97

Rangers no longer rule – OK! Fired up Celtic finally smashed the Light Blue domination of these recent Old Firm clashes in devastating fashion last night.
Ally Guthrie, Daily Star, enjoys Celtic's Scottish Cup Quarter-final victory over the Ibrox side in March 97

Today I have to do something I rarely had to do before – give the Rangers fans an APOLOGY. Our cup performance at Parkhead on Thursday was nothing less than shocking. Inept. Sloppy. Second-rate...It was the WORST Rangers performance in an Old Firm game I've ever experienced.
Ally McCoist, News of the World, March 97

GAZ'S FOOL

Midfield magician Paul Gascoigne is here to give you an alternative guide to footie fitness. First things first and perfecting your ball skills (left) is a must if you want to be like Gazza – remembering to look your best at all times! Next, suss out your team-mates' opinion with a subtle question; "So, am I good or am I good?" asks Gazza (below). "Nice grass this…" says Bo and Tommy.

RACE YOU... Nothing like a bit of competition – especially if you can beat a certain record-breaking Ranger...

GUIDE TO FITNESS

Sit-ups (left) are essential for that perfect footballer six pack – plus make sure you keep a hand in everything (right)

RICHARD GOUGH once said that the team which drinks together and play together , wins together. If that's the case then the inspirational Rangers skipper must be the best social organiser British football has ever seen.

Gough's influence on the park has held many an Ibrox defence together over a decade, while his ability to motivate and galvanise a squad off the pitch helped give Rangers the best dressing room spirit in the country throughout Nine-in-a-row.

Although Gough felt passionately about his decision to seek a new life in the United States because he feared he would be playing for Rangers while past his peak, he soon discovered there was no where quite like Ibrox.

Kansas City Wizards were the most improved team in the Major League Soccer under his guidance but Gough's heart was elsewhere – back home in Scotland.

So it was a dream come true when Walter Smith made the move to bring back the player he has been closest to throughout his managerial career. The news spread smiles across the Atlantic Ocean from America's mid-west to every Rangers fan on the other side, including Scott Nisbet whose game flourished while playing alongside Gough in the early Nineties.

"Some people talked about this being a backward step, but these people have short memories," said Nisbet. "Goughie was and still is absolute top quality.

"Never mind his age, it's fitness and hunger that counts. His appetite for winning is astonishing and his fitness would put anybody playing in the Scottish game to shame.

"He was our captain on and off the park. Often if we didn't have a game in midweek he would book a table in

THERE'S NO PLACE LIKE HOME

A tribute to a Rangers great by Fraser Mackie

restaurant and make sure we all went for lunch together. That's where team spirit is moulded."

That type of togetherness was never better demonstrated than in the unforgettable and unbeaten Champions League run of 1992/93. Another battle-hardened star of those days, Mark Hateley, did 'a Goughie' himself last season by answering an emergency call from Smith.

So he's one of the few men who can understand how Gough felt after leaving the club he loves.

"He's probably realised what he's been missing," explained Hateley. "Going to America when he did possibly wasn't the right decision, but everyone can look back with the benefit of hindsight.

"He'd been at Ibrox for 10 years and it's understandable why he felt in need of a change.

"His leadership qualities are his best assets and he's a rock in defence.

But it was the concern that he would not be able to give Rangers that level every week that persuaded Gough to make the tough decision to quit Scotland for a new challenge.

At the European Super Sixes tournament in the Amsterdam Arena, Gough met with the legendary Italian defender, Franco Baresi of AC Milan.

"Baresi was an example of what I was scared of," confessed Gough. "He was playing in an AC Milan team when he shouldn't have been.

"He was 37, just off the pace and they were losing games like 6-1 to Juventus. Walter Smith was at that game and told me he was just a yard away from everything.

"It'd be a terrible blow for a man of his standing, a man with his pride, to suffer that."

Yet such is Gough's remarkable durability that he could remain at the very top of his profession for several years to come.

"His reading of the game is second to none," insisted John Brown who formed a true Braveheart partnership at the centre of the Rangers defence for two years.

"The amount of covering work he does is a tremendous asset to any team. Everyone he plays alongside appreciates just how good a player he is, although he often doesn't get the credit he deserves.

"He has been a major player in the club's success and has won a tremendous amount of trophies as captain. He's a great leader."

And lead he will, with Ten-in-a-row the next goal – an ambition Goughie thought was impossible for him when he walked out the Ibrox doors in tears last May.

"He was our captain on and off the park"

OLD FIRM

In every one of his first nine seasons with the Gers, Ally McCoist scored at least once against Celtic.

Rangers' first shirt sponsor was CR Smith, whose association with the club began in 1984 – at the same time as Celtic.

Rangers' 5-1 demolition of Celtic in August 1988 was their biggest victory in the fixture for 28 years.

Up until the start of the current season, Rangers have been involved in more European matches, playing 174 times to Celtic's 149 ties.

It's well known that Celtic now play in green and white hoops – but did you know Rangers used to play in blue and white hoops – and Celtic in green and white vertical stripes?

The boys in blue recorded their first-ever Premier League victory at Parkhead on August 23, 1980. Goals from Alex Miller and Jim Bett gave the Gers faithful two reasons to be cheerful.

The first ever Old Firm match was a 'friendly' in May 1888. Unfortunately, Celtic won 5-2. While the first league clash in March 21, 1891 produced a 2-2 draw.

THE OLD FIRM AMAZINGLY DID NOT MEET IN A SCOTTISH CUP FINAL BETWEEN 1928 AND 1963.

Jim Baxter was certainly a lucky charm for the Teddy Bears! Appearing in 18 Old Firm games between 1960 and 1965, Jim was only on the losing side twice and he often joked that he received letters from the wives of Celtic fans, thanking him for making sure their husbands were home early from the game!

Rangers and Celtic are two of the best supported clubs in the world and feature in the list of top 10 season ticket sales in Europe.

30 facts on the world's best game

Rangers are well ahead in the League Cup stakes with an impressive 20 victories to Celtic's nine.

Rangers have th upper hand when it comes to league titles, winning an incredible 47 championships to Celtic's 35. But Celtic gain revenge in the Scottish Cup – winning 30 cups to the Ibrox men's 27.

RANGERS WERE FORMED BEFORE CELTIC, BEGINNING IN 1873 – 15 YEARS BEFORE THEIR EAST END RIVALS.

Rangers' record attendance at Ibrox came in 1939 when 118,567 fans squeezed into the ground for the Old Firm clash.

Celtic's record came the previous year when they managed to cram 92,000 into Parkhead against Rangers.

Rangers' clean sweep of victories against Celtic last season was the first time either of the Old Firm had won all the derby encounters since the Premier League began.

Unbelievable though it seems, the Celtic support actually cheered a Rangers goal during an Old Firm encounter at Hampden in September 1972. With their team strolling to a 3-0 win, the bhoys showed their appreciation of a last minute John Greig consolation goal.

Following the Ibrox disaster of 1971 when 66 Rangers fans died, an Old Firm Select played Scotland in aid of the fund. George Best of Manchester United guest starred – and scored – for the select side.

Both clubs have achieved glory in Europe, with Rangers clinching the European Cup Winners' Cup in 1972, while Celtic carried off the European Cup in 1967.

OLD FIRM

30 facts on the world's best fixture

Although he stole all the headlines in 1989, Mo Johnston isn't the only player to have turned out for the blue and the green. In days gone by, Tom Dunbar, William Kivlichan, Alfie Conn and George T Livingston are just a few who made the bold move.

The great rivals have met on 13 occasions in the Scottish Cup Final since their first meeting in 1893. Rangers have triumphed five times, while Celtic have won seven...

...The odd one out was the Scottish Cup Final in 1908/09 when the cup was witheld after a riot broke out.

A brave man, Tom 'Tiny' Wharton refereed an astounding 23 Old Firm matches during his career.

There's no surer way for a new boy blue to endear himself to the Ibrox faithful than to score his first goal for the club in an Old Firm derby. Richard Gough, Nigel Spackman, Terry Hurlock, Alex Cleland – and not forgetting Paul Gascoigne! – are just a few players who've managed the feat.

Rangers have had nine managers in their history to Celtic's 10 with both Jock Wallace and Billy McNeil having double stints at Ibrox and Parkhead respectively.

Hampden has been the temporary home of both Rangers and Celtic. While Ibrox was being reconstructed in season 78-79 the Gers played their derby home games at the national stadium recording a 1-0 victory and 1-1 draw with the Celts. Season 94-95 saw the Parkhead team take on the Gers twice at Hampden suffering a 3-1 defeat in October, thanks to Hateley and Laudrup, but running out 3-0 winners in the last Old Firm clash of the season.

Up until the start of the season the highest scoring Old Firm match was the enthralling 4-4 game on 22 March, 1986. A double from Cammy Fraser plus strikes from Ally McCoist and Robert Fleck made up the Gers four goal tally.

January 1982 to April 1984 was the longest spell the bears have ever had without an Old Firm win. A goal from Bobby Williamson ended an eight game barren spell.

The Gers are no strangers to unbeaten derby runs and have twice managed to go 13 Old Firm League games without defeat from 1922-28 and 1957-64.

In a 5-1 win at Parkhead in September, 1960, the Gers heroes netted four goals in 25 minutes.

WINNER TAKES IT ALL

"For me, there's no argument about when Nine was won. That came at Celtic Park back in March.

"Mark Hateley had been whisked back to Ibrox and I remember all the Celtic fans laughing their heads off, saying they were going to destroy us.

"But as we walked to the game, our support was singing 'There's only one Mark Hateley' and I just *knew* it was going to be our day.

"Sure enough, their defence couldn't handle big Mark and the Danish Prince did it again – what a day!"

JULIE CLARK,
KIRKINTILLOCH

"I just knew it was going to be our day"

THE JUDGE

Ally McCoist talks to Keith Jackso

Marco Negri received a lot of publicity at the start of the season for not smiling – but believe me this man LOVES scoring goals.

"That's how he sees his job description – simply to put the ball in the net. The man is frightening and he's my kind of striker.

"He scores goals with his head, he scores them on the volley, he scores with chips and he scores them with his knee from one yard out. The man is a goal machine. I know there were a lot of rumours about him not being happy at the club because of his lack of celebrations but that's nonsense.

"He's the first one to say good morning when you go in for training and his face lights up. He loves the banter and, although he doesn't take part in most of it, you can see him almost wetting himself if something funny is going on.

"I really like the guy and I'm convinced he would score goals for any team in the world. It'll be very interesting to see just how many he's scored come May."

"Marco's face lights up when we go into training in the morning"

"Rino Gattuso's enthusiasm for the game gives everyone a lift"

Rino is the Duracell of the dressing room. If you get into the ground early enough you often see him and Stuart McCall plugging themselves into the mains and getting charged up for training!

"Together they are the groundsman's worst nightmare. They notched up a record of 84 slide tackles in a single training session.

"The fans have fallen in love with the wee man and it's easy to see why. They love his enthusiasm for the game and the fact that he will NEVER give up. He's very similar to Stuart McCall in that respect.

"He's actually more like a traditional Scottish midfielder than an Italian because of the hunger he shows and his willingness to run for every lost cause.

"That kind of enthusiasm is infectious and it gives everyone a lift.

"His English is coming on nicely but it's still bad enough to be funny – which is much the same as Ian Ferguson's!"

"I'll be the man running on with the sponge when Seb returns!"

"Tony is known as the country boy of Ibrox!"

Big Tony Vidmar takes a lot of stick in the dressing room and being Australian he warrants it. Tony and Craig Moore are known as the country boys or the bumpkins of Ibrox but they take it well.

"Tony can also dish it out and, like the rest of the new boys, has settled into the dressing room really well.

"Charlie Miller gave him the nickname Viddy the Diddy – and that's about the only funny thing Chalire has come up with in his entire time at the club!

"Unfortunely, Tony suffered a little at the start of the season because he was forced to play in the middle of the defence when he is really a left-back.

"But he has a lot of qualities and is another sound investment for the club."

Seb Rozental is officially the nicest man in the world and everyone is dying to see him come back from injury and do well for the club.

"It's so depressing seeing him go into the weights room every morning when we go training. I've been there and you feel like throwing up.

"But Seb will be back and when he is he'll become a real favourite of the fans. They really took to him when he first arrived and they will again when he is back playing.

"He's not an out and out frontman like Marco – he'll probably play a bit deeper and link up more with the midfield – but he'll score his fair of goals.

"Mind you, I'm not sure what I'll be doing when Seb's back in business – maybe I'll be the guy running on with the sponge!"

TURN OVER FOR ALLY'S THOUGHTS ON THE REST OF THE IBROX NEW BOYS →

COISTY GIVES HIS VERDICT ON GERS' SUMMER SIGNINGS

THE JUDGE

Ally McCoist talks to Keith Jacksc

"ANTTI IS AFTER GORAM'S SHIRT"

Antti Niemi, like many of the new guys, has had his fair share of injury problems since signing but I really like the look of the big man.

"If there's one thing a goalkeeper needs it's confidence and Antti has bags of the stuff. He's good and he knows it and he's never scared to give his defence a rollocking when they need it.

"He also has a real physical presence about him and is the sort who really commands his area.

"He is also very highly respected on the international circuit because of his performances for Finland and he has not come here just to make up the numbers – he's after Andy Goram's shirt.

"It really is the first time in recent years that Andy has had a serious challenger for the position and it'll be interesting to see how that battle turns out."

I really felt sorry for Jonas Thern after our defeat in Gothenburg when he was quoted as having a bit of a pop at the rest of the lads.

"We all realise that sometimes you can be taken out of context over things like that – especially when it's translated back into English.

"In truth we knew he wouldn't have done us in – but it didn't stop us getting right into him the first time he walked back into the Ibrox dressing room.

"In fact, Paul Gascoigne went straight up to him and said: "The sooner you realise the only reason you were brought here was to do my running the better it'll be for everyone!"

"But Jonas is a magic lad and he took it all in good spirit. He's very like Brian Laudrup as a shining

"Thern will be a great player for the club"

example of the complete professional but he still likes a good laugh with the rest of us. Mind you, he tends to give Charlie Miller a lot of stick so he picks on the easy targets.

"Jonas also struggled at the start of the season as he was playing with a knee injury and you could see he was annoyed by it. He was angry that he wasn't starting off his Rangers career at full tilt.

"But make no mistake – this guy is a GREAT player and will prove it."

can quite definitely say that Staale Stensaas is one of the fittest players at this club. The boy is a machine!

"Unfortunately, he arrived here as the replacement for David Robertson and that was always going to be an unenviable task as Robbo was such a favourite with the fans and had such a good understanding on the left with Lauders.

"But Staale has come in and quietly got about the job.

"He's scored a couple himself and has shown that he can add to the team in attack as well as defence. Staale is another who has played at a very high level in Europe with Rosenborg and it's good to bring in players with that kind of experience behind them."

Sergio Porrini came in for a bit of criticism when he first arrived but this guy is quality – believe me.

"You just have to watch him in training to see that he has been schooled at the very highest level with Juventus.

"He trains the way he plays – with real aggression and passion. Believe me, he's a big strong boy and, as a striker, it's always good to be in his side rather than up against him.

"The belief seems to be that guys like Porrini are only in it for the money. Well, I've seen this guy in close quarters and I can assure everyone that is not the case. He realises Rangers are a massive club and he really WANTS to do well here."

> **"You just have to watch Sergio in training to see he's top quality"**

"Lorenzo has a real passion for the club already"

Lorenzo Amoruso is a brilliant lad and I feel so sorry for him. He's been desperate to start playing for Rangers but his Achilles injury has left him on the sidelines and it's really hurting him. At times the poor guy has looked soul destroyed by it all.

"But he'll get over it and when he does he'll be a superb player for us. He was brought here as Richard Gough's replacement and I believe he has all the same qualities that made Goughie such a hero.

"He has a presence about him and he looks the sort who can dominate a defence.

"He also has a real passion for the club already despite the fact he's only played in two pre-season games. He comes to watch every game, home and away, and enjoys the company of the players.

"It's a terrible shame to see him sitting things out for so long but he'll be back and when he is it will have been well worth the wait."

> **"STENSAAS IS A MACHINE!"**

COISTY GIVES HIS VERDICT ON GERS' SUMMER SIGNINGS

DISCOVER THE PERSON BEHIND THE PLAYER AS WE GO... STAR

ARIES

From: 20 March – 19 April
Player: Jonas Thern
Date of birth: 20 March 1967

There's nothing Aries the ram likes more than a challenge – and Jonas fits that bill perfectly! Alert, active and adaptable, this guy always uses his head to guide his feet producing the midfield mainstay that we all know and love. Born leaders, Ariens love to overcome obstacles and opposition.
Warning! – He hates to lose.
Other Ariens – Andy Goram (13 April, 1964)

TAURUS
From: 20 April – 20 May
Player: Peter Van Vossen
D/O/B: 21 April 1968

Once in action a Taurean is hard to stop – so Scottish defenders beware! Mr V's sign is as stubborn as a bull and once he's figured out exactly what he wants he'll charge right in to make sure he gets it (unless it's a goal at Celtic Park, that is!). Solid and dependable, Taureans have tremendous strength and endurance as Peter has shown with his direct running at defences.
Warning! – He'll never admit he's wrong.

GEMINI

From: 21 May – 20 June
Player: Paul Gascoigne
D/O/B: 27 May 1967

Active, clever, skilful, versatile – and often totally unpredictable! Sound vaguely familiar? Yes, Gazza is the perfect Gemini. The social butterfly of the zodiac, the Geordie genius loves to be the centre of attention and rarely runs out of things to say but when he does he lets his feet do the talking.
Warning! – The Gemini twin has the attention span of a fly!
Other Geminis – Antti Niemi (31 May 1972), Stuart McCall (10 June 1964)

CANCER
From: 21 June – 22 July
Player: Derek McInnes
D/O/B: 5 July 1971

The sign of success a Cancerian can make it all the way to the top. Home-loving and helpful this man is totally trustworthy and dependable – which is exactly the midfield role Del boy plays every time he's asked to pull on the blue jersey at his beloved Ibrox home.
Warning! – Beware the many moods of the Crab.
Other Cancerians – Lorenzo Amoruso (28 June 1971), Tony Vidmar (4 July 1970), Alan McLaren (4 July 1971), Staale Stensaas (7 July 1971)

LEO

From: 23 July – 22 August
Player: Gordan Petric
D/O/B: 30 July 1969

Leo the lion is ambitious, confident and loves to lead the way – essential qualities for a Rangers defender. An expert in emergencies, Gordan Petric is the ideal man to have around Ibrox as the casualty list grows bigger every day.
Warning! – Can sometimes be a bit of a bossy boots...

VIRGO
From: 23 August – 22 September
Player: Sebastian Rozental
D/O/B: 1 September 1976

Quick-minded and on the ball is Virgo man Seb. The ultimate perfectionist, self-belief is one of Virgos' greatest traits. This man will never give up and he's prepared to work until he drops – which is music to the ears of the Ibrox support.
Warning! – Virgos love to get their own way.
Other Virgos – Stephen Wright (27 August 1971)

GAZING

LIBRA

From: 23 September – 22 October
Player: Ally McCoist
D/O/B: 24 September 1962

A Libran possesses amazing intuition and can recognise good from bad instantly – so that explains the sensational scoring habits of old king goals Mr McCoist! Alert and always prepared, Super Ally trusts his instincts and as he's shown time and again for the Gers if something's worth fighting for he'll be there giving it his all.
Warning! – Laid back Libra finds time-keeping a little tricky…

SCORPIO

From: 23 October – 21 November
Player: Marco Negri
D/O/B: 27 October 1970

Just like the Scorpion, this guy is quick and sharp in attack. A shrewd, fearless fighter, Negri can size up situations no-one else can and knows instinctively when to deliver his sting – and break the hearts of the Premier defences!
Warning! – You never quite know where you are with the enigmatic Scorpio.
Other Scorpios – Ian Durrant (29 October 1966), Sergio Porrini (8 November 1968), Erik Bo Andersen (14 November 1970)

SAGITTARIUS

From: 22 November – 21 December
Player: Gordon Durie
D/O/B: 6 December 1965

The sign of the archer, this sharp shooter NEVER misses his mark. Full of enthusiasm and filled with vision, Jukebox can do anything he sets his mind to. Concentration is the key to his success which explains the furrowed brow as Jukey makes his way into the penalty box.
Warning! – He can be Mr Clumsy at times!
Other Ibrox Sagittarians – Theo Snelders (7 December 1963), Alex Cleland (10 December 1970), Craig Moore (12 December 1915)

CAPRICORN

From: 22 December – 19 January
Player: Rino Gattuso
D/O/B: 9 January 1978

One of the finest signs of the zodiac, a Capricorn thrives on responsibility and is destined to break into the big time – making little Rino the perfect man for the Gers midfield. Solid and determined, Gattuso will NEVER accept defeat and his passion for the game enables him to renew his energy and rise to even greater heights.
Warning! – It takes a while to gain the trust of a Capricorn.

AQUARIUS

From: 20 January – 18 February
Player: Jorg Albertz
D/O/B: 29 January 1971

In tip-top condition, Aquarians are fit, healthy and strong – as The Hammer has proved with his 70 mph free-kicks! Able to turn their hand to anything, this sign loves to please and is happiest when helping others – like laying on Erik Bo's two wonder strikes in the New Year Old Firm Derby of 1997!
Warning! – You'll often find him drifting off into a world of his own…
Other Ibrox Aquarians – Barry Ferguson (2 February 1978)

PISCES

From: 20 February – 19 March
Player: Brian Laudrup
D/O/B: 22 February 1969

Pisces stands for perfection – and what better way to describe our Prince of Denmark? Possessing skill and imagination, he'll fight against all the odds – which Lauders has done repeatedly during his Ibrox reign. When things fall apart, there's no better person to have around than a Pisces.
Warning! – Has a tendency to get a little restless…
Other Pisces – Joachim Bjorklund (15 March 1971), Ian Ferguson (15 March 1967), Charlie Miller (18 March 1976)

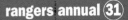

NON-STOP McCALL

Ten things you never knew about... STUART McCALL

May 15, 1993, was the proud moment when Stuart first wore the Rangers captain's armband. Brockville was the venue, Falkirk were the opposition and the Gers were the winners. A 2-1 victory was a fine result for the stand-in skipper and he loved every minute: "Being captain is thoroughly enjoyable and a great honour."

Stu says falling over the ball against Aberdeen in season 1993/94 to let Duncan Shearer score was his most embarrassing moment ever!

His first international call-up was at Valley Parade – for England under-21s! Thankfully for Scotland he stayed on the bench or he might just have been Stuart McCall of England.

The best thing about being a footballer for Stuart is "doing something I'd always dreamed of doing and also the day to day banter in the dressing room".

McCall certainly played his part in nine-in-a-row turning out an impressive 159 times since his arrival from Everton in 1991 and weighing in with 15 goals.

Steve Martin and Meg Ryan are Stu's favourite actor and actress while Andre Agassi is his top sportsman!

When asked his best ever moments Stuart doesn't have to think twice: "I've got magic memories of beating Celtic twice with 10 men and the Leeds United games."

Stuart's stay in Scotland has certainly been a succesful one – he's won six League Championships, three Scottish Cups and two League Cups!

During his stint at Everton, the midfield maestro was brought on as a sub during the 1989 FA Cup Final against Merseyside rivals Liverpool – and scored twice! Unfortunately for Stu an FA Cup medal eluded him when Liverpool hit back, thanks to Ian Rush, and lifted the cup with a 3-2 win after extra time.

Simply The Best or anything by Ocean Colour Scene come top of his pops!

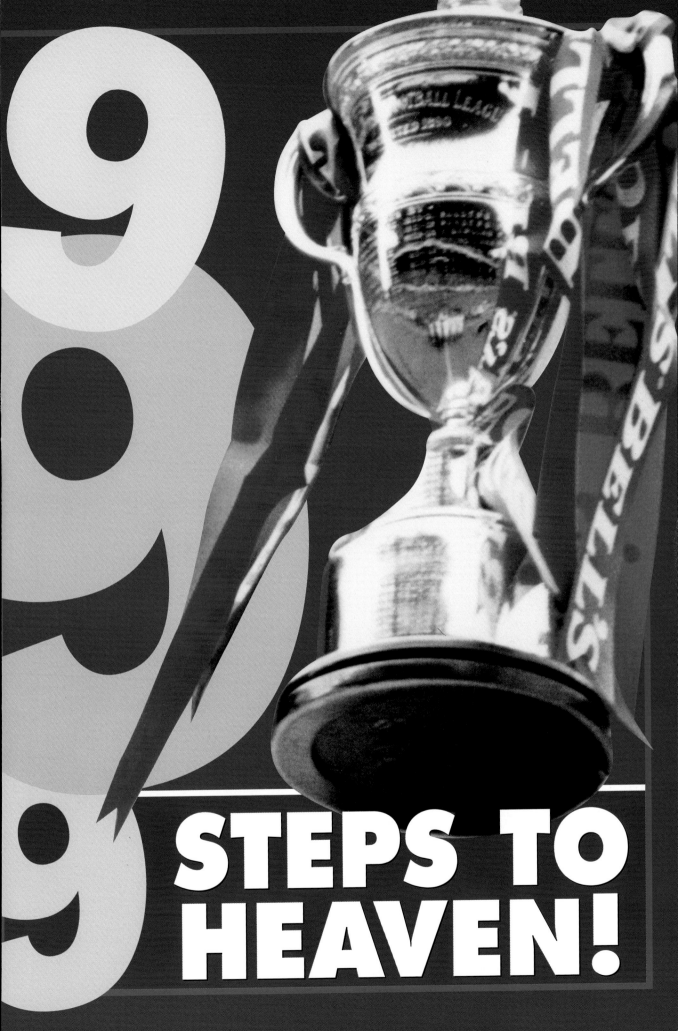

99

STEPS TO
HEAVEN!

THE LEGE[N]
NINE-IN-A

W alter Smith – a man who keeps his emotions bubbling under the surface – sped from the Tannadice dugout and leapt on top of his players' famous huddle.

That was just one of the images from the unforgettable night of May 7, 1997 that summed up just what nine-in-a-row meant to Rangers.

Click the camera shutter on to the moment when the trophy that has become the club's personal property was presented to Richard Gough.

The skipper – whose courage and guts had made him one of only three Ibrox players alongside Ian Ferguson and Ally McCoist to win those nine title medals on the trot – burst into tears.

His American adventure with Kansas City Wizards was about to begin and Gough knew this looked like the end of an era. But he was walking out the door the way he'll always be remembered at Ibrox. A winner.

Matching Celtic's historic run of championship successes will live with every fan who witnessed that season for the rest of their life. Gough's pride at being the captain when it happened will always burn inside him and he said: "I knew I was leaving a legacy as captain of Rangers.

"I'd won more trophies than any other Ibrox skipper and that was always going to give someone a lot to live up to.

"But I don't think that was simply down to Richard Gough.

By IAIN KING, Chief Sports Writer, The Sunday Mail and author of 9 – the officia[l] story of nine-in-a-row

It was down to the sheer success o[f] the past years."

Gough, Ferguson and McCoist [are] three men who had been th[e] backbone of a run that made the[m] legends.

Three men of vastly differen[t] characters and vastly varying skills[.] But three men who will alway[s] hold one thing in common – the[y] are all true Rangers men.

Fergie has often found him[-] self the target of the boo-boy[s] at Ibrox yet his devotion to th[e] club is unquestioned.

The Gers have been able to count on his combative skills in midfield for nine years now since Graeme Souness paid St Mirren £850,000 to land the player who'd grown up as a Rangers-daft kid in the shadow of Parkhead!

And Fergie smiled: "Sure, there have been dark days when I had troubles with illness and injury but I'm proud to be in that trio. Try the question on your friends. Name the three players who won all the medals in nine-in-a-row? I bet my name doesn't spring to mind immediately.

"But I've been there through it all and I'm proud of that."

The last word from three players who have earned a special place in the hearts

GIVE US A HUDDLE... The boys in blue celebrate their 1-0 win at Celtic Park which completed a unique Grand Slam of Old Firm league victories

DS OF -ROW

9

...of the faithful who pack Ibrox every week must go to the man who shyly has MBE stitched on his training gear – Ally McCoist.

It's bizarre to remember these days that Jock Wallace once told a struggling McCoist he could speak to CARDIFF CITY if he wanted to find a way out of Ibrox.

And, serious for once, Ally said: "No matter what happened in my bad times at Rangers nothing has ever shaken me from the belief that I can score goals for this club."

Writing the official story of the club's title triumphs, *9* dragged me down Memory Lane with the stars who made it happen.

One idea for a chapter that never quite happened was the Nine-in-a-row Dream Team...

TURN OVER FOR MORE

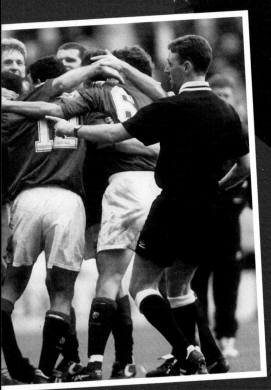

Now the *Official Rangers Annual* gives me the chance to indulge myself and cause a million arguments as you ask the question bawled at me in Press Boxes throughout Scotland: "Whit gemme were you at?"

Well, here goes. I get an unlimited transfer budget and the scope to pick players from all nine triumphs.

Surely, I'd have no disputes about my first choice **ANDY GORAM**: The Goalie – as he is simply known around Ibrox – is, in my mind, the top keeper in Europe on his day.

How many times down the years have you seen him beaten one on one with a striker clean through? It doesn't happen often.

Celtic boss Tommy Burns summed up what Andy means to Rangers when he famously said: "My tombstone will read: 'Here he lies, Goram broke his heart.'"

GARY STEVENS is my right-back in a four-man defence because he was very close to the perfect modern-day man on the flank.

A superb athlete, his final cross did let him down at times but very few got past him and he often chipped in with vital goals.

On the left would be **DAVID ROBERTSON** and Staale Stensaas will already know the void he is trying to fill.

A constant threat going forward and his pace at the back often covered for the lack of acceleration of players like Richard Gough and Alan McLaren – another who shone going forward in a Gers side that dominated so many games.

My centre-halves picked themselves, **RICHARD GOUGH** and **TERRY BUTCHER**.

Gough's relationship with the Rangers fans has always puzzled me. They realised his class but never really seemed to idolise him the way they did Tel.

Yet to me he was just behind John Greig as the greatest Rangers captain.

He said when he left after nine-in-a-row that he would miss the Gers more than they would miss him. He was wrong.

Butcher was the perfect match with that left peg pinging 60-yard passes and his skill was so often under-rated.

There's no question of his

A TRUE
DREAM

commitment as he battered dressing-room doors off the hinges at Pittodrie and Parkhead after defeats!

To my mind he was THE Souness signing that really sparked the rebirth of Rangers in 1986. In midfield I have the chance to pick four men who for me encapsulate why Rangers fans fork out for season tickets every year – they do things with the ball mere mortals could only dream of.

First of all **RAY WILKINS**. Although he was in the autumn of his glittering career when he made it to the Gers he still remains one of the best passers of the ball ever to grace the Light Blue.

He left the pitch in tears when he finally quit to head back south but while he was here there were so many days to savour. His legacy lives on in the likes of Ian Ferguson who constantly sought advice from a man who saw it all with England and some of Europe's finest sides including AC Milan.

Beside him would be **PAUL GASCOIGNE**, a flawed genius but a genius all the same who won the club's eighth successive title almost single-handedly with a hat-trick in a dramatic 3-1 win over Aberdeen.

Luring Gazza from Lazio remains one of the great coups of the Walter Smith era.

The other, and without doubt the best, Smith heist was **BRIAN LAUDRUP** for £2.25 million from Fiorentina. Go to the High Court any week and you'll see people jailed for less serious robberies than that.

Laudrup is, quite simply, the best player I have EVER seen in a Rangers jersey. His balance and vision have been a joy to watch over the years.

When he leaves – and it's inevitable in the new age of football that he will – he will leave a massive gap to be plugged in the fans' affections.

There just had to be a place finally in the middle of the park for **IAN DURRANT**.

Unquestionably the player of his generation until he was cruelly cut down by Neil Simpson's tackle at Pittodrie on October 8, 1988.

It was to cost him almost three years of his career yet he still came back to be a star in the Champions League run in 1993.

I believe he would have fulfilled Souness' prediction and made it in Italy but for that numbing setback.

Up front teams thrive on partnerships and there has been none better for the Ibrox side than **MARK HATELEY** and **ALLY MCCOIST**.

It took a while for Hateley to win over the fans but becoming the man who haunted Celtic and scoring the title winning goals in season 90/91 certainly helped!

Fearsome in full flight, he was born to partner a predator like McCoist.

Behind the smiles with Ally lies a cold-hearted penalty box killer who preys on half a chance.

Memories are too many to mention for him. He's very old now and, at 35, is due a longer contract from *Question of Sport* than the next one he'll get at Ibrox!

Still who could forget the overhead kick that won the League Cup against Hibs in 1993 on his comeback from a broken leg? Typical McCoist.

So that's my verdict and whatever you think, one thing's for sure; every player who played a part in Nine-in-a-row made football history.

Well, my stint as a manager is over, there's a Mr Smith at my door…

BLUE TEAM

STRIPPED
AND READY FOR ACTION

1996-97: The second strip of the season, it certainly played its part in the Light Blues historic nine-in-a-row season. The team produced fine 5-2 and 3-0 wins over Dunfermline plus a 4-1 victory over Kilmarnock and the unforgettable 6-0 demolition of Raith Rovers wearing their away day kit!

1996-97: The boys' first pulled on this strip in the magnificent Scottish Cup Final of 1996 with great success. A dazzling display by Laudrup – and two superb goals – plus a hat-trick from Gordon Durie saw the Gers defeat Hearts 5-1 at Hampden.

1994-96: Two of Smith's greatest signings made their Ibrox League debuts wearing this Adidas strip. Danish king Brian Laudrup donned it for a 2-1 win over Motherwell back in 94 while Gazza played his part in a 4-0 demolition of Raith Rovers in September 95.

1993-94: A break from the traditional red, white and blue this second strip certainly had the fans split in two but it was good enough for one of the Gers biggest signings. Duncan Ferguson joined the Ibrox side in 1993 for a record £4 million from Dundee United and the 6ft plus striker was proud to pull on the orange and blue jersey!

1992-94: Undoubtedly one of the most successful strips in the Gers history, the boys in blue lifted two Premier Leagues, two Scottish Cups and two League cups wearing this lucky Adidas strip – and the fifth Scottish Treble in the club's history.

1992-93: This kit will no doubt remind most fans of the Euro dream that almost came true. Who could forget Pieter Huistra's superb strike against Club Brugge or the sheer joy on true blue Ian Durrant's face when he netted in the Velodrome against Marseille as the Gers came within a whisker of the European Cup Final?

1990-92: Ibrox Stadium, May 11, 1991, was probably the most memorable day of this kit's lifetime. As one of the tightest championships in history came to a climax with a showdown against challengers Aberdeen, Mark Hateley saved the day for the Gers with a deadly double to keep the Championship flag at Ibrox.

1988-90: When the team pulled on this jersey way back in 1988 little did they know they were taking the first step towards a piece of Rangers history – the first leg of nine-in-a-row. It also witnessed the departure of two of the finest players ever to grace the Ibrox turf as both Ray Wilkins and the late, great Davie Cooper bid their farewells to the Ibrox support.

1984-88: An old favourite, this Umbro kit was paraded to the footballing world in 1986 when Graeme Souness arrived at Ibrox – and began the Scottish football revolution. As the English invasion began with the arrival of Terry Butcher and Chris Woods the Light Blues scooped their first League Championship in nine years.

They say life begins at 40 for some people, but for Rangers maverick genius Paul Gascoigne his has begun a decade early – his quiet life that is.

The most talked about footballer of his generation has courted controversy since the day he pulled on a black and white shirt for boyhood heroes Newcastle 10 years ago.

Never had such a young man had to deal with such a weight of expectation, or intrusion, as the public eye followed him to London and then onto Rome as his career panned out.

At times it became too much as the pressure blew up in Gazza's face, before Walter Smith pulled off the most audacious piece of transfer business in his managerial career, to bring the playe to Scotland at a cost of £4.3 million.

Unfortunately for the Geordie the firs two years of his life in Glasgow brough no respite.

Not even 36 goals in 72 games as he helped Rangers to two championships and the coveted nine-in-a-row landmark could appease his critics.

Some adverse publicity was self-inflicted, but Gascoigne only ever appeared to be at ease when he was performing on the pitch.

But now, halfway through his third term at Ibrox, the midfielder is beginning to discover that it's his football that is now making the headlines.

Paul turned 30 in his time with England at Le Tournoi last summer. So-called experts labelled it a threshold for the Rangers ace, a crossroads in his career that could not afford to take another wrong turning.

Thankfully for Gazza, and for football, i appears he has followed the right path.

Gascoigne has emerged as a controlled and focussed character, a man on a mission to see out the rest of his days at the top level. It came as no co-incidence

"I am in the fans' blood – and they are in mine

hat his re-vamp came after a new three ear contract with Rangers.

Gazza is a man who responds to aith. Walter Smith put it in him, David Murray put it in him, and when he feels wanted, Gascoigne is content.

That happiness has brought us a new character, still the same old cheeky smile and wisecracking Gazza, but underneath that facade a man that at last feels he is n charge of his own destiny.

"Walter Smith was the man who gave ne my life back," admits Gazza, "I had over 40 operations in my time in Italy

and he came and signed me which meant a lot to me.

"Both him and the chairman have stuck by me and when I was offered a new contract I had no hesitation signing.

"Ideally I would like to end my career at Ibrox. I am in the Rangers fans' blood and they are in mine.

"This is a massive club, as big as they come and I am desperate to continue to enjoy the success I've had here."

And as Rangers career towards a new year, there is no doubt the unique talents of Gascoigne will play a major part.

The bid for a record making tenth consecutive title will continue to remain priority and Gazza will be at the helm.

"I don't bother what people say about me any more," he smiled, "I know I will get slaughtered if I don't have a good game. But it's what the people who matter to me think that counts.

"We live with the pressure that we are expected to win every game but that can spur you on.

"Getting 10-in-a-row is what we want and we'll all be going for it, I can assure you of that."

NEW TEAM NEW PAUL

GAZZA'S DERBY CHEER

"The first Old Firm game of the season was my highlight of the nine-in-a-row campaign.

"It was my first derby and the atmosphere was just unbelievable. I'd never experienced anything like it in my life.

"And when Richard Gough put us ahead just after half-time I went mental!

"But that was nothing compared to the celebrations in the stands when Gazza put us 2-0 up seconds after Celtic had hit the bar.

"I'll never forget that moment as long as I live."

BILLY WOODS, PERTH

"I'll never forget that moment as long as I live"

● After a 4-3 defeat from Dundee in August 92, this Rangers team embarked on an incredible run of 44 unbeaten games in all competitions.

● Against all the odds, the lads of '92 defeated English champs Leeds United 2-1, both home and away, and notched up an impressive 10 unbeaten matches in their 1992-93 European Cup run.

● This remarkable team completed the Scottish Treble – a feat only four other Rangers teams had managed to achieve.

THEY SCOOPED THE TREBLE, THEY CONQUERED EUROPE, THEY WERE

SIMPLY THE BEST

SIMPLY

andy goram

Still Rangers' number one. The keeper was outstanding during the famous Champions' League run and has kept up that sparkling form with great displays season after season.

richard gough

The captain of the team remained at Ibrox to lead his troops to the marvellous achievement of Nine-in-a-row before deciding to head for pastures new, in the shape of American Major Soccer League side Kansas City Wiz. But the call of Ibrox was too much for Richard and he returned in October to solve a defensive crisis.

scott nisbet

Cult hero Nissy will forever be remembered for the amazing goal that secured Rangers' 2-1 Champions' League win over Bruges at Ibrox. Likeable Nisbet never managed to establish himself as a first team regular, but it was a knee injury that ended his career tragically early. He is now a sales rep for a leading sportswear manufacturer.

david robertson

The speedy left-back went on to give Rangers another four excellent seasons before leaving the club in the summer. Robbo claimed he was bored with the Scottish League and signed for Premiership aces Leeds, where he is now an established first-team regular.

dave mcpherson

Slim was an unsung hero of the 1992/93 team and often unfairly criticised by pundits and punters. McPherson moved to Hearts from Ibrox for the second time in October 1994 as part of the deal that took Alan McLaren to Rangers. He has provided the Tynecastle's young side with the experience they need and has become a firm fans' favourite.

john brown

Bomber arrived at Ibrox in 1988 and never failed to produce full-blooded performances for the team. Another who didn't often receive the credit he deserved, Brown's talents were recognised by Rangers, as he is now on the coaching staff, working with the reserve and youth players.

ian durrant

Durrant was spellbinding in the Champions' League run and notched spectacular goals against Club Bruges and Marseille. Unfortunately, the most talented Ranger of his generation has continued to suffer injury problems, but he remains an important member of the first team squad.

ian ferguson

Fergie handed Rangers their first Champions' League win when his goal defeated CSKA Moscow in Berlin. That was just one of the former St Mirren man's vital

SIMPLY THE BEST SIMPLY

CONQUERED EUROPE, THEY WERE

THE BEST

MARK WILSON TAKES A LOOK AT THE SIDE THAT HELPED MAKE HISTORY

contributions that year and he continues to turn in top class displays in the Ibrox engine room.

trevor steven

Silky Trev had just rejoined the club for £2.4 million after a season in France with Marseille, who splashed out £5.5 million for his talents.

The England international scored a rare headed goal to win the Ne'er Day clash with Celtic in 92/93, but suffered from a series of injuries in the following seasons.

He was released by Rangers at the end of the season and is now a regular media pundit.

alexei mikhailitchenko

The Ukranian midfielder was the enigma of the 1992/93 team. He turned in supreme shows one week only to be anonymous in a game just days later. Unfortunately, Miko's career was blighted by injury, and he was released by Rangers in 1995. Alexei had a brief spell in England with Charlton, but is now on the coaching staff of his first club, Dynamo Kiev.

pieter huistra

The Dutch winger sparkled in the Champions' League and scored a crucial equaliser in the away tie with Bruges. He left Ibrox early in 1995 for a spell with Japanese side Sanfreece Hiroshima. He returned to his homeland with Groningen, but is now starring for Belgian champs Lierse.

mark hateley

The Hateley-McCoist partnership went from strength to strength in 1992/93 as the English ace netted 19 league goals. Mark left Ibrox for QPR three years later but returned briefly to help injury-stricken Rangers to Nine-in-a-row. He is now manager of English Third Division side Hull City, with fellow Ger Billy Kirkwood as his assistant.

ally mccoist

Super Ally netted twice against Leeds and scored a remarkable 34 league goals in 1992/93. He then went on to break just about every record in Rangers' goalscoring history to guarantee his place in the club's folklore. He may be 35 now but no-one in their right mind would write off Coisty's chances of grabbing a few more vital goals for the Light Blues.

THE BEST SIMPLY THE BEST

1 Who scored Rangers first goal of the nine campaign way back in August 88?

2 Which three players have winners' medals for all nine seasons?

3 Name the nine goalkeepers who wore the number one jersey.

4 Which player made the most appearances for all nine seasons?

5 Ally McCoist finished top of the nine goal scoring chart – but who came second?

6 What was the Gers biggest victory of nine, who was their opponents and in which season did it happen?

7 Who was the only team to knock four goals past the Gers?

8 Which Sky TV personality turned out for the Gers in season 88/89?

9 Which four players did Rangers sign from Dundee United?

10 What made the Old Firm League clashes of season 96/97 unique?

11 Which Ranger was an ever present in the eight-in-a-row season?

12 What were the four teams that finished runners-up to the Gers during nine?

13 Name the two full-backs signed from Aberdeen.

14 Who were the three Irishmen to wear the Light Blue?

15 Against which team did Rangers clinch three-in-a-row and who scored the goals?

16 The Gers had an amazing run of victories in season 92/93 – how many Premier League games did they remain undefeated?

17 How many Premier League games did the boys in blue lose during eight-in-a-row – and which teams did the damage?

18 What profit did the Ibrox side make when they sold Trevor Steven to Marseille in 1991?

DO YOU KNOW

FIND OUT WITH OUR

QUESTION 10...
Brian Laudrup has been a sensation for Rangers and takes particular pleasure scoring against Celtic – do you know what made last year's Old Firm League meetings so special?

19 During season 90/91, two teams could not put the ball in the Gers net in all four league encounters – can you name them?

20 Ally McCoist was captain for the first time in September 92 – can you name the opposition?

21 Three players signed from Everton during nine – can you name them?

22 Who scored the two goals for Motherwell which spoiled the Ibrox party in May 97?

the Gers made three signings who were all Scottish – can you name them?

28 Rangers visited Brockville for the last game of season 92/93. Can you remember the score – and who wore the captain's armband for the first time?

29 Can you name the two players who played in every game during season 90/91?

30 Who scored the final goal of season 96/97?

9-IN-A-ROW?

QUIZ FOR ALL SEASONS...

23 Rangers beat Hearts 3-0 at Ibrox in September 96 but another incident grabbed the headlines – what was it?

24 Can you name the four teams who defeated the Gers at Ibrox during six-in-a-row?

25 Who scored the winning goal of the New Year Derby of season 89/90?

26 Where did Rangers clinch eight-in-a-row and who scored the goals?

27 During one close season

ANSWERS

30. Derek McInnes
29. Gary Stevens, Chris Woods
28. 2-1, Stuart McCall
Wishart
27. Gordon Durie, Duncan Ferguson, Fraser
26. Ibrox, Paul Gascoigne
25. Nigel Spackman
Motherwell
24. Celtic, Dundee United, Kilmarnock,
Pointon, Paul Ritchie
players – Pasquale Bruno, David Weir, Neil
23. Referee Gerry Evans sent off four Hearts
22. Owen Coyle
21. Stuart McCall, Trevor Steven, Gary Stevens
20. Dundee United
19. Hibernian, St Mirren
18. £4 million
17. Three – Hearts (2), Hibernian
16. 29
15. Aberdeen, Mark Hateley
14. Darren Fitzgerald, Jimmy Nicholl, John Morrow
13. Davie Robertson, Stephen Wright
12. Aberdeen, Celtic, Hearts, Motherwell
11. Alan McLaren
encounters
first ever Grand Slam of Old Firm Premier League
10. The Gers won all four games making it the
Gordan Petric
9. Gary Bollan, Alex Cleland, Duncan Ferguson,
8. Andy Gray
7. Dundee
6. 7-0, Hibs, 1995/96
5. Mark Hateley
4. Richard Gough
Woods
Billy Thomson, Nicky Walker, Chris
Maxwell, Colin Scott, Theo Sneiders,
Ginzburg, Andy Goram, Ally
3. Andy Dibble, Bonni
McCoist, Ian Ferguson
2. Richard Gough, Ally
1. Gary Stevens

ALEX CLELAND

Alex Cleland's qualities as a footballer have never been in question.

However, it took the vast majority of the Rangers faithful a long time to realise his full worth to the team.

Not because they didn't want to like him – simply because he did his job so quietly and efficiently that no-one seemed to notice. Cleland, signed from Dundee

United in 1993, has slotted in alongside a host of top international stars at Ibrox and NEVER looked out of place.

The past 18 months must qualify as Cleland's finest in the game and he will be a valued member of Walter's squad for a long time to come.

IAN FERGUSON

Highly-paid, skilful players come and go from football clubs like the average fair-weather fan. That is a football fact.

It is not often in these days of soccer mercenaries that a man will shed blood for the cause.

Ian Ferguson, however, is one man who has seen and done it all before at Ibrox – and would run through brick walls to do it all again.

Never has the term 'playing for the jersey' been more apt for a player. Fergie is blue through and through.

Thankfully, he has the skills to back up this commendable attitude.

Putting in a power of work in midfield, Fergie's never-ending enthusiasm is a vital part of his play – as are his power packed free-kicks.

With 17 winners medals in his collection from a glorious time at Ibrox, including all nine-in-a-row medals, no-one can question his value to the squad's remarkable success over the past few years.

UNSUNG HEROES

Paul Gascoigne, Alexei Mikhailitchenko, Trevor Steven and Brian Laudrup. All names which trip off the tongue as silky, creative Rangers playmakers of the past six years.

There is one, often unmentioned, common denominator among these players – Stuart McCall.

The tigerish tackling and powerful running of the little man have laid the engine-room platform for many ball players to show their quality.

It is said that every good team must earn the right to play football by winning the battle in the early stages.

McCall has been a midfield master at this, triumphing in the battle to leave the way clear for his highly skilled team-mates. All of this is not designed to cloud McCall's own qualities.

He has scored a fair share of goals and provided a mixture of classy passes to create others throughout the years and is truly one of the games' unsung heroes

STUART McCALL

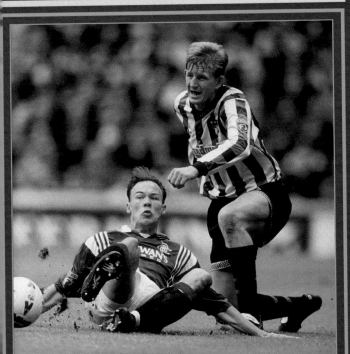

JOACHIM BJORKLUND

Joachim Bjorklund has become something of a quiet achiever during his spell at Ibrox.

Signed in time for the famous nine-in-a-row campaign, the Swedish international has gone about his business in a typical, low-key Scandinavian fashion.

Like all good players from that part of the world, Bjorklund isn't the type to grab headlines.

His cultured style of defending isn't the type to set a fan's

pulse racing. No wild tackles on the opposition's glamour boy or clenched fists to team-mates.

Bjorklund is best known for his superb speed. He slots into the central defensive position and confidently struts his stuff in a manner which goes largely unnoticed by the supporters – but it is certainly noticed by Walter Smith who has made Jocky a regular.

...FIRST RANGERS ENCOUNTER

"I used to play for my school, Hunter High, in East Kilbride and lots of clubs used to come and watch us play. one of those games we drew 5-5 and scored four goals! One of the spectator was the Rangers scout, George Runcima and he arranged for me to go to Ibrox an have a chat with Willie Thornton. But th day before I was due to go, St Johnston offered me signing terms and I accepted

"Over the years people have said I' turned down Rangers but it's not true! was only going to Ibrox that day to mee Willie Thornton NOT to sign for the Gers.

...WEARING THE BLUE JERSEY

"Playing for Rangers is a fairytale com true. My dad took me to my first Ranger game when I was nine and it's been m ambition to play for them ever since."

...HIS FAVOURITE GOAL

"If I had to choose I would go for m goal against Celtic in he 1991/92 Scottish Cup semi-final.

"We played most of the game with 10 men after Davie Robertson wa sent off and although we were under tremendous pressure throughout the game, we man aged to hold out for a famous 1 0 victory."

...BRIAN LAUDRUP

"It's great playing along side people like Laudrup and Gazza and, being a striker, it's brilliant to know that if you make a run you'll get the ball back or it'll find someone else in a better position.

"During the nine-in-a-row

> **The fans have been brilliant to me throughout my career, apart from a few early hiccups and I know nine-in-a-row meant so much to them.**

season Laudrup was out of this world and some of his performances were on another planet. His contribution outwith his goals has been unbelievable, in fact, you end up running out of superlatives to describe him!"

...THE FANS

"The fans have been brilliant to me, apart from a few early hiccups and I know nine meant so much to them.

"The atmosphere at Tannadice the night we won nine was incredible and when the fans started chanting my name while I was warming up it really brought home to me how much I wanted to win it for them."

...THE BEST THING ABOUT BEING A FOOTBALLER

"It's got to be scoring goals. It feels absolutely fantastic and puts you on such a high.

"But I never feel above the rest of the team – if I did I wouldn't last two minutes in the dressing room!"

...BREAKING RECORDS

"I always like to set targets for myself and I'm not giving up.

"I feel great and want to score as many goals as possible – and as long as I don't embarrass myself or the club, I'll keep on going."

> **"The atmosphere at Old Firm games is second to none. Every time I score against Celtic it gives me more pleasure than any other goal."**

...THE OLD FIRM EXPERIENCE

"The atmosphere is second to none and the feeling's still the same as the very first time. When you run out the tunnel against Celtic all you think about is winning.

"To score is amazing because what you are doing is scoring for the team you supported as a boy against their biggest rivals.

"So every time you score you are fulfiling a dream – it gives me more pleasure than any other goal.

...FAVOURITE OLD FIRM GAME

"The League Cup Final in March 84 was probably my outstanding one because it was my first major cup final. We won 3-2 after extra time and with me scoring a hat-trick, getting booked and then giving away a penalty for their equaliser in normal time made it quite an interesting day!"

...HIS SPARE TIME

"Music is where I go when I need to escape from all the pressure. Springsteen and Bon Jovi are my favourites. If there's football on TV I'll watch it and tapes of myself playing – not out of vanity but to study the moves and chances I should have taken."

> **"If I had a pound for every time I was told I was finished I'd be a multi-millionaire. I've taken some amazing stick from so-called experts."**

...CRYING

"At the end of the CSKA Moscow game in 1993, I broke down on the pitch. I took a look at our packed stand, awash with red, white and blue and the singing from our fabulous support put a huge lump in my throat. The emotion was too much for me and I can assure you those tears were for real. It wasn't the first time I'd cried on the Ibrox pitch either. When we beat Aberdeen 2-0 on the last game of season 1990/91 to clinch the championship I was reduced to tears – I was extremely proud to be a Rangers player that day."

...NINE-IN-A-ROW

"It was something I'd dreamt about for a long time and to be part of it was magnificent.

"It meant a great deal to me and guys like Goughie, Fergie, Bomber and Durranty who've been at the club throughout the nine-in-a-row run and, being diehard Bluenoses, equalling Celtic's feat is extra special. You just had to look at Goughie's face when he was presented with the trophy at Tannadice to see how much it meant to him."

...THE END OF MCCOIST THE FOOTBALLER?

"If I had a pound for every time I was told I was finished I'd be a multi-millionaire. I've taken some amazing stick and flak from the so-called experts but my record speaks for itself. I am resigned to the fact I am coming to the end of my career but I feel there is still a lot left in me yet."

COISTY
THE IBROX HERO SPEAKS

CHASING THE BIG TIME BREAKTHROUGH

MICHELLE SIMPSON chats to up and coming pair Steven Boyack and Darren Fitzgerald about fighting their way to the top...

WHEN DID YOU FIRST PLAY FOOTBALL?

STEVEN: According to my dad I was only two-years-old when he gave me a ball to kick about in the back garden – although I have my doubts! I played for a couple of local sides, Carse Thistle and Riverside Boys Club, when I was about nine.

DARREN: I was nine and I remember playing with all the older boys out in the field by my house – and nearly beating them! When I was 11 years old I joined up with St Andrews Boys Club in Belfast and I was with them right up until I signed for Rangers.

WHEN DID YOU JOIN THE GERS?

STEVEN: I joined the Gers' schoolboys when I was 14 but I didn't actually go full-time with Rangers till July 93. I signed on for two years which is the usual deal offered to the young boys who make it.

DARREN: It was July 94 before I signed on. Even though I was on the Rangers books I still played in Belfast until I was 16 and ready to make the move. I must admit it was pretty upsetting leaving all my friends and family back in Belfast.

WHAT WAS IT LIKE MIXING WITH THE FIRST TEAM?

STEVEN: It was strange at first because I'd cheered a lot of them on as a fan but they all made me feel really welcome – particularly the Scottish boys.

DARREN: To me Ally McCoist is a legend so it was slightly scary in the beginning. Derek McInnes and Ian Durrant are really down to earth and great for helping all the young lads out.

DID YOU HAVE TO WAIT LONG FOR YOUR FIRST TEAM DEBUT?

STEVEN: I was a substitute against Steaua Bucharest and Clydebank before I finally got my moment in October 96.

DARREN: I'd been here nearly three years when I was a sub against Kilmarnock in March 97.

HOW DID IT FEEL?

STEVEN: It was strange because I felt nervous but I also had a funny sense of relief that I was finally getting my chance. Unfortunately it wasn't the best of games as we went down 2-0 to Hibs and Laudrup missed two penalties!

DARREN: My game wasn't much better – a 2-1 defeat at Ibrox! I got on the park for half-an-hour and I remember my heart was racing as I ran on but after a few touches I settled into the game.

DO YOU EVER GET THE CHANCE TO TRAVEL WITH THE TEAM?

STEVEN: I've been in the squad for several of Rangers' European away games so I've had the chance to visit a few countries. The Vladikavkaz game in Russia was the worst place I've ever been to. There was only one hotel which had a security guard on every level – and we had to take our own bedding with us!

DARREN: I've not been involved with the first team as much as Steven but I have been to Germany with the youths – and our pre-season tour of Northern Ireland is always a winner!

"Our main aim is to play for the first team regularly"

WHAT'S BEEN THE BEST MOMENT OF YOUR CAREER SO FAR?

STEVEN: Obviously my first team debut was a special moment but there was also a brilliant Glasgow Cup Final against Celtic when I was 18. We won 3-1 and I had a hand in all the goals – and of course we beat our Old Firm rivals which made it even better!

DARREN: I played in a brilliant Glasgow Cup Final a few seasons ago – funnily enough it was against Celtic too! We won 1-0 and I scored the winning goal which was a brilliant moment. I suppose playing alongside Coisty in the first team wasn't too bad a moment either!

WOULD YOU SAY YOU'VE BEEN SUCCESSFUL AT RANGERS?

STEVEN: Well, I've won one Premier Reserve League, three Glasgow Cups, two BP Cups and three Reserve League West medals but, to be honest, the main aim of every professional footballer is to play for the first team regularly – it's the only way to judge how successful you are.

DARREN: I think Steven's right. I've won about four medals here which isn't bad but playing for the top team is what it's all about – but we've still got plenty of time to make that step up.

ANY TIPS FOR ALL THE WOULD-BE RANGERS STARS OUT THERE?

STEVEN: I'd recommend they find a good Boys Club because the Rangers scouts are always out and about watching games. Apart from that just work hard and spend a lot of time working with the ball practising your skills.

DARREN: All you can do is try your best and remember to enjoy it. The day you stop enjoying football is the day to give up.

MICHAEL STONE

Date of birth: 15/1/79
Birthplace: Stirling
Position: Defender
Signed: January 94 from Gairdoch United Boys Club
Favourite Player: Paul Gascoigne
Fact: Stone was in the first team squad that travelled to the Faroe Islands to play Gotu – and was almost picked after injuries to Craig Moore and Tony Vidmar

MAURICE ROSS

Date of birth: 3/2/81
Birthplace: Dundee
Position: Defender
Signed: July 97 from Fairmuir Boys Club
Favourite Player: Paul Gascoigne
Fact: His ambition is to make the grade at Rangers – and he'd love to meet pop star Louise!

MICHAEL RAE

Date of birth: 24/11/76
Birthplace: Inverness
Position: Goalkeeper
Signed: July 94 from Ross County
Favourite Player: Andy Goram and George Weah
Fact: Michael is currently the fourth choice keeper at Ibrox – but says he can only improve with the help of Andy Goram, Antti Niemi and Theo Snelders

STAR

DAVID YOUNG

Date of birth: 1/3/79
Birthplace: Glasgow
Signed: July 1995 from Rangers SABC
Position: Midfield
Fact: David was out injured for an amazing 14-month-spell and made a goal-scoring comeback against Dunfermline in September

BARRY NICHOLSON

Date of birth: 24/8/78
Birthplace: Dumfries
Position: Midfield
Signed: May 95 from Maxwellton Thistle Boys Club
Favourite Player: Paul Gascoigne

Fact: When Barry first featured for the Rangers youths' his hair was dyed WHITE!

JIMMY GIBSON

Date of birth: 19/2/80
Birthplace: Bellshill
Position: Midfield
Signed: December 95 from Mill United Boys Club
Favourite Player: Paul Gascoigne
Fact: Jimmy would love to be capped for Scotland – and he's a big fan of rock group Bon Jovi!

ROBERT MALCOLM

Date of birth: 12/11/80
Birthplace: Glasgow
Postion: Defender/Midfielder
Signed: December 1996 from Rangers SABC
Favourite player: Ian Durrant
Fact: Robert skippered the Gers youth side in their first match of the season against Stenhousemuir – and fired Rangers into the lead with a cracking volley

KIRK WILLOUGHBY

Date of birth: 28/1/81
Birthplace: Cambridge
Position: Defender
Signed: December 96 from Hillwood Boys Club
Favourite Player: Franco Baresi
Fact: Kirk would love to win a European medal with the Gers and reckons he would have become a lawyer if he hadn't made it as a footballer

MAKING

DAVID GRAHAM

Date of birth: 6/10/78
Birthplace: Edinburgh
Position: Forward
Signed: July 95 from Rangers SABC
Favourite Player: Ally McCoist and Ronaldo
Fact: David won his first Scotland U-21 cap in September v Belarus

STEPHEN CARSON

Date of birth: 6/10/80
Birthplace: Ballymoney
Position: Forward
Favourite player: Brian Laudrup
Signed: July 1997 from St Andrews BC
Fact: Stephen made his first team debut when he came on to replace his hero Brian Laudrup at the Nike Family Day

PETER MacDONALD

Date of birth: 17/11/80
Birthplace: Glasgow
Position: Forward
Signed: December 96 from Hillwood Boys Club
Fact: Peter's biggest game to date has been in a testimonial for Morton's David Wylie. In a team packed with big names, Peter upstaged them all with both goals in a 2-0 win

BETTER THAN ALL THE REST

From Dunfermline to Dundee, Auxerre to Amsterdam the Rangers loyal legions are guaranteed to follow follow in their thousands. Their constant backing and support play a vital part in the team's success and they certainly know how to show off their colours! As our pictures show nine-in-a-row was every fans' dream and they can be sure of one thing – the Gers will be giving their all to deliver 10!

COISTY'S SIMPLY THE VEST

"The Grasshopper game at Ibrox was one of my highlights of last season.

"Things had been so bleak for us in Europe that I was half dreading going to the game that night.

"So when Ally put away the penalty in the second half then added a second I was jumping up and down like a madman!

"Honestly, you'd think we'd just won the European Cup with my reaction. I think part of it was out of sheer relief that we'd managed to gain a win but, also, Ally had given us all just a little bit of our pride back – cheers Ally."

CRAIG JOHNSON,
MOTHERWELL

"You'd think we'd just won the European Cup"

SEASON 1997-98 RANGERS